This book belongs to

~~Noelle Nielling~~

Children's
POOLBEG

A Paperback Original
First published 1990 by
Poolbeg Press Ltd
Knocksedan House,
Swords, Co Dublin, Ireland

© Michael Comyns 1990

ISBN 1 85371 117 9

Poolbeg Press receives financial assistance from The Arts
Council/An Chomhairle Ealaíon, Ireland

Cover design by Carol Betera
Illustrated by Carol Betera
Set by Richard Parfrey
Printed by Nørhaven Rotation, Viborg, Denmark

The Trouble with Marrows

The Trouble with Marrows

and Other Whimsy

Michael Comyns

**Illustrations by
Carol Betera**

Children's
POOLBEG

For

Natasha, Charlotte and Zoe,
In support of the proposition
that
One pound of Tommyrot
Equals a quart of Hogwash
Or 2.5 (metric) Fiddlesticks

Contents

The Trouble with Marrows

Alternative Treatments

Private Lives

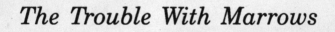

The Trouble With Marrows

Skinks

In Syria's sands and other warm lands
Live charming small lizards called SKINKS.
That unfortunate name, for which they're
                              not to blame,
Is the cause of much mirth and high-jinks.

Who laughs at the lynx or smirks like a sphinx
At the mention of elk or g-nu?
And I'd shrink from a mink,
Wouldn't you?

Let nobody think that the skunk and the skink
Are one and the same class of mammal.
It's the skunk makes the stink and the
                              innocent skink
That must dodge the flat feet of the camel.

The Hidebehind Gogwoggle

There's a Hidebehind Gogwoggle under your
bed.
No, that isn't dust...it's the hair that it's shed.
But you'll never see it whatever you do
For it moves very quickly and hides behind
YOU.

There's a Hidebehind Gogwoggle just at your
heel.
No you'll never see it though sometimes you'll
feel
It make holes in your sock with its fingernail
Or hear the swish of its scaly tail.

The Hidebehind Gogwoggle carries a sack
As it searches the room behind your back
And the thing you can't find though you had it
last night
Has been grabbed by the Gogwoggle just for
spite.

The Hidebehind Gogwoggle slams the door
And scatters peas on the dining-room floor.
It cracks the cups and spills the glue
But it can't be caught. It hides behind YOU.

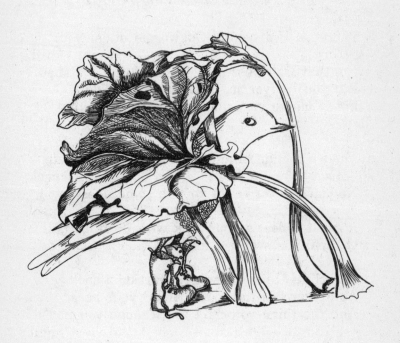

The Prune Bird

Unlike the seal and conger eel
The Prune Bird has no song,
But in his mouldy hockey boots
Creeps quietly along.

He builds no nest. His woolly vest
Is all he ever wears.
He sleeps amongst the rhubarb roots
Where he is safe from bears.

The two, you see, cannot agree
On whether flies rise early,
Or how to pickle bamboo shoots,
And what makes cabbage curly.

Departed Spirits

It seems that ghosts are going out of style.
I haven't seen or heard one for a while.
No rattling of bones.
No wailing, clanks or groans.
No disembodied heads with toothy smile.

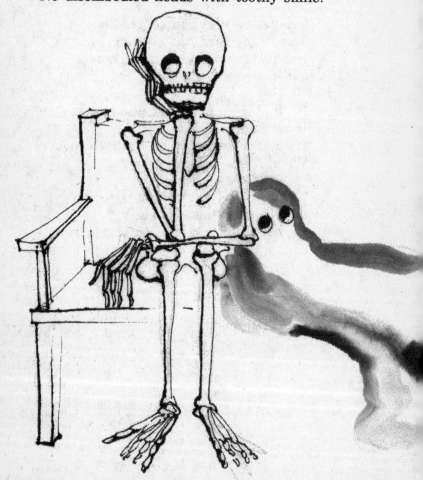

I haven't met a bogey man for ages.
Perhaps they're all on strike for higher wages.
Haunting ruined towers,
Working such unsocial hours,
Doubtless puts them into polterghastly rages.

It's hard to get a ghoul these days. I've tried
To hire a vampire or spectral bride.
So haunting's up for tender
And phantoms (any gender)
May apply. All balls and chains supplied.

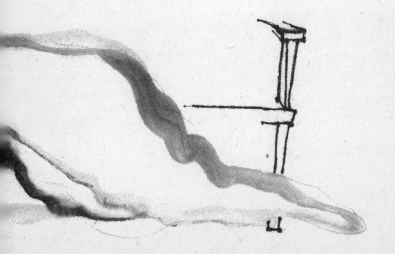

Eine Kleine Mölmusik

Buzzing bees are bad enough
And so are cats that sing
But a mole that plays the trumpet
The most irritating thing!

I'd forgive his horrid habit
Of eating slugs and snails
If he'd confine himself to that
Instead of playing scales.

I'd ignore the tiny tunnels
And the lumps upon the lawn
But now he's brought a cousin in
Who plays the flugelhorn.

The latest news is worse again.
He mentioned, quite offhand,
That moles throughout the parish
Are to form a German band.

They're playing Souza night and day.
Some fifty four at least.
They must be prosecuted
For Disturbance of the Peace.

I've told the village policeman
And he says that he will come
When the woodworm in his truncheon
Has stopped practising his drum.

Cautious Cows

Cautious cows. Shy, fearful
Neurasthenic, timid, tearful,
Very seldom wag their tails.
Often bite their fingernails

Good Egg

The egg's a spiritual creature
And temperance its endearing feature
Unlike the riotous runner bean
A rowdy egg is never seen.

The egg lets other people be
Except for acts of charity
Like sending pots of marmalade
And seeing that the bed is made.

Most evenings the eggs stays home
And darns his socks or reads a poem
And when the daylight's growing dim
He'll close his eyes and hum a hymn.

The Trouble With Marrows

The trouble with marrows (and certain courgettes)
Is their habit of keeping tin kettles as pets.
For a tin kettle's all very well in its place
But not on my lap or licking my face.
And they snap at the postman and moult on the
                                        chairs
And leave their disgusting bones on the stairs.
Now one is drinking the ink from my pen.
I shall never share rooms with a marrow again.

Tribute To Gumboot

Humble and all as the Wellington boot is
It never neglects its Christian duties.
It visits sick neighbours and waters the flowers
And plays with the children for hours and hours.

It cleans their teeth and washes their faces
And never trumps its partner's aces.
It's certain to see that the cat is fed
And NEVER NEVER smokes in bed.

A Wellington boot is a comfort at night
For it closes the windows and turns out the light.
It quenches the fire and bolts the doors...
We must forgive the fact that it snores.

Fireworks

The spotted newt or salamander
Admits with admirable candour
That in spite of legend he
Knows nothing of pyrolgy.
In fact he finds that sudden heat
Causes chilblains on his feet.

Though sometimes while he's in the bath
He warms his slippers in the hearth.

Alternative Treatments

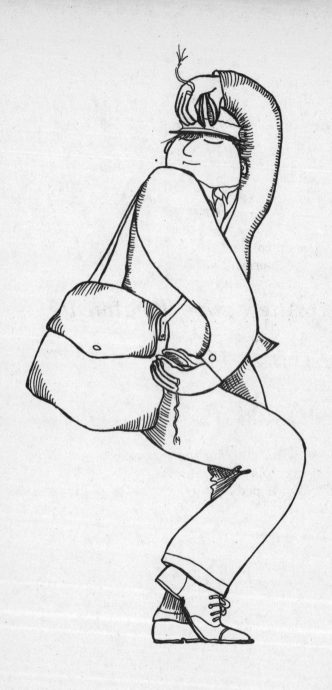

Mail Order

I intend to send away,
By the morning post today,
For an aeroplane that works by oil combustion,

For an ex-Swiss Army bike
That my gardener would like
And a pair of castenets with full instructions.

When the postman comes at last,
No doubt as in the past,
He will weigh up what the situation needs.

While I'm starting the propeller
He may play a tarantella
And we'll pedal round the roses pulling weeds.

Who Cares?

What has it got to do with you
If I spread my escalopes with glue?
Why in the world would anyone care
If I wore a geranium in my hair?

Why care a toss or even a fig
If I dress my bloodhound in a gown and wig?
If I push my butler in a bath-chair
It's really none of your affair!

I'll hop where I please on my pogo-stick
And wrap my mothballs in candlewick.
Should I post my aunt to Kalamazoo
It's really nothing to do with you.

Rules Rule—OK?

Private car park.
Members only.
Please keep off the grass.

Call the sheriff.
Form a posse.
Stop them at the pass!

Thin red line.
Heart of oak.
All salute the flag.

Squad, Attention!
Boots and saddles.
Catch the scallywag!

Breakfast Menu

I don't care for eggs and bacon
Till my porridge has been taken
With a pint or two of tea to wash it down

Then I like my rashers crispy
With a drip or two of dip. Please
Try to fry the eggs till their petticoats are brown.

Should the toast have butter melted,
Or be cold, al dente, well bred
Sort of toast with Cooper's Oxford marmalade?

Then perhaps a pot of coffee
(Blue Mountain) a brioche. We
Must have a bite of something while the plans for
                          lunch are made.

Banco Ezio

The Governors of the Bank declare
That if you leave your money there
For long enough and them some more,
And are not tempted to withdraw
A single sou for any reason,
On quarter day and in good season,
Barring earthquake, fire or folly,
Inflation, staggers, melancholy,
Occurrences of Cosmic Nature,
Crises in the Legislature,
Strikes incited by detractors
And all IMPONDERABLE FACTORS,

If you and cash are kept apart
You'll have as much as at the start.

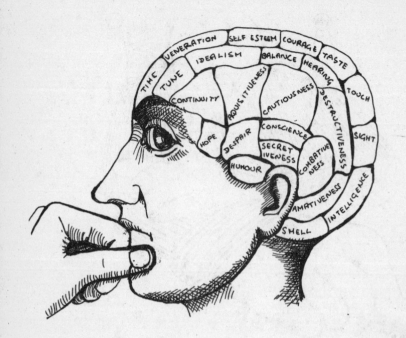

Alternative Treatments

Phrenology, a useful science that
Tells us what goes on and where beneath the hat.
Check your bumps out on the chart.
We can list 'em part by part,
Then practise Mesmerism on the cat.

Acupuncture too. Looks fun to me.
Where can I find a patient who'll agree
That a pimple on the nose
Calls for tintacks in the toes.
If he can't afford to pay, I'll do it free.

Aromatherapy...No, can you guess?
A healing snort of eau-de-watercress.
Offer guests your potted flora
For a gin and angostura
Is not a half as likely to impress.

There is really very little room for doubt,
Psychiatrists can well be done without.
If your brains are out of tune
It's the phases of the moon.
Have you tried the port-and-beefsteak cure for gout?

The Toffee Mine

Invest in toffee mines? I hear
That's not all a good idea.
It's there in tons, oh right enough,
But how to shift the beastly stuff.
In any kind of warmish weather
One's pick and shovel stick together.
No sooner do the miners start
Than tools must all be licked apart.
Just think of all the time it takes
And all the awful tummy aches.
And not just that...it clogs the hair,
Eyebrows, fingers, everywhere.
It clogs your socks, your boots, your laces.
It gets in most unlikely places.
Imagine if you can, the smell
Of mint, vanilla, caramel.
And on a sticky summer's day
The fumes would make you swoon away.

How sad the toffee miner's lot,
To have such wealth yet have it not.
He guards his hoard but lives in doubt
That he will ever get it out.

Lost Property

Somewhere here around
There's a cavern underground
And I've never ever found its entrance yet.

I can't say exactly where,
Haven't got a clue to share,
But its crammed with underwear, my pet. You bet.

I've been tearing up the floor
And what exactly for
I'll explain. It's plain. It has been found by others.

Maybe south-south-east of Hell
There is God's Own Deepest Well
Where all left-footed socks shall meet their brothers.

Belovēd Leader

There is only one solution:
We must have a revolution
And I will help to build the barricades.

Fetch my red paint. Just a dab'll
Rouse a regiment of rabble.
And we'll send them off to face the fusilades.

No cowardly cad or funker
Is allowed inside my bunker.
If the shooting's done I'll come and take a bow.

When we've purified the system
If there's wronguns left we've missed 'em,
But never fear...I'll run the show from now.

Nursery Rhyme

Corn crake. Fenny Snake.
Give a dog a bone.
Leave our planet
Very much alone.

Forced march. Spray starch.
Give a man a gun.
Off to fight a battle.
Tremendous fun!

Fast Food. Lassitude.
Give a guy a dime.
Nineteen-ninety
Nursery Rhyme.

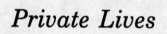

Private Lives

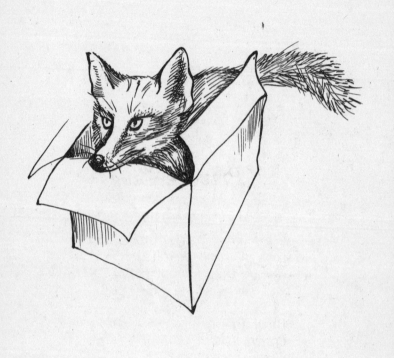

Happy Family

Billy Blossom hunts for foxes
Packs them into cardboard boxes
Takes them to the railway station
Sends them to a near relation
Living in the Isle of Wight.

Mrs Blossom knits pyjamas
Posts them to the far Bahamas
Cousin Rose from Talahassie
Makes them out of papier maché
But she isn't very bright.

Baby Blossom sings a ditty
Of the fish that built the city
Crystal seaweed, rubber chairs,
Mongeese, battle cries and bears
Till the early morning light.

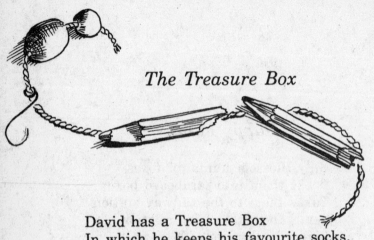

The Treasure Box

David has a Treasure Box
In which he keeps his favourite socks,
Almost a half a tube of glue,
A stone that has a hole right through,
Some pencil ends, for who knows when
They might come in for use again,
Three fish hooks and a leaden thing,
A necessary piece of string,
Five beads, two shells, a feather that
He thought might look well in a hat,
A watch that goes in fits and starts
(Though it has nearly all its parts)
A nail file and some lemon drops—
Not good, but enough for swaps.

Private Lives

Giaramolo Savonarola
Often played the pianola.

Pierre Etienne Theodore Rousseau
Dressed himself from mother's trousseau.

Sir Hyram Stevens Maxim
Never let his problems tax him.

Friedrich Carl Von Savigny
Said he didn't have any.

Alexander Graham Bell
Used to kiss but never tell.

Nicolo Paganini
Did of course...the meany.

Patrick, Who Heeded His Parents'
Wishes
And GOT ON

It was young Pat's misfortune that
His parents owned a city flat
Where, naturally, they would not let
Him keep a dog to be his pet.
Instead, they said, content yourself
With goldfish kept upon a shelf.

The years went by and Pat grew up
And still he longed to own a pup.
His folks worked hard and then retired.
In time they peacefully expired.
The price of flats in Dublin 4,
Pat found, had just begun to soar.

So promptly, through an old school chum,
He sold up for a goodly sum.
At once he bought a house and grounds.
Now he is Master of the Hounds.
The goldfish too, applaud the change
Whilst swimming round his moated grange.

Foreign Affairs

Did you know that Turks and Jews
Dance with porridge in their shoes ?

Did you know Bulgars and Greeks
Have two Thursdays in their weeks?

Poles eat moles.When gypsies fiddle
They play their tunes from end to middle.

Only Englishmen think rightly—
They change their bedsocks three times nightly.

Brace Yourself

Delia's teeth are bent and bucked
Despite the costly silver bracket,
But she can pick a chop or eat
An apple through a tennis racquet.

The McGoos

On the coast of Timbuctoo
Where the fun and games are few
And the turtles seldom flap a flippant flipper

Lives Archibald McGoo
And Mrs McGoo too
And they do not welcome tourist, tramp or tripper.

They sit upon the strand
Like the lords of all the land
And it's every piece of bladderwrack and jetsam

Oh I beg you, don't enquire
If their deckchairs are for hire
For the commonplace or mundane merely frets 'em.

Be it morning, noon or night
They like to do things right
And wear the proper dress for each occasion.

Because they're very wise
They take daily exercise
And are of a vegetarian persuasion.

Watch them walk along the pier
From the far end to the near
And back again but never see the sea.

It's because it goes away
At about this time of day
And returns at five to four in time for tea.

Executive Igloo

In the quieter part of Ballsbridge
An Eskimo lives in a fridge.
It's crowded in there
With a polar bear,
A kayak,
Twelve dogs
And his
Sledge.

Good Scout

I think I shall be an explorer
And own a telescope,
A lamp and a helical borer,
A leather trunk and a rope.

I'll cock my topee at the ready,
My hammock and compass full tilt.
I'll pack my toothbrush and Teddy.
And for evening dress...a kilt.

I'll travel by mule and by ferry,
By llama and dinghy and yak.
I'll risk yellow jack, beriberi
And a bad cold before I get back.

If I don't return before sundown
I'll hardly be home before dark.
Would you bring me some tea and a bun down
           To my camp in Dollymount Park?

I See No Professorships

He is always in his study.
He's a ruddy fuddy-duddy.
He drinks only hand-picked herb tisane.

And now and then emerges
To distil his daily purges
From the rhizome of a young Dogsliverbane,

Instead of explanation
He will write a dissertation
And recite it over supper if you like.

If your views should vary slightly
He will not regard it lightly
And you'll get a double dose tomorrow night.

He's a purist eight times purer
Than the nudest nature curer
So I beg you not to disagree.

For he'll write his version down,
Acquire another hood and gown
And increase his reputation...one degree.

Cruncher Sparrow High Flier
by
Gordon Snell

Cruncher Sparrow, flying high.
Looked for adventure in the sky.
He met a host of other birds,
Had friendly chats and fighting words;
He tried to race and chase and swoop—
He even tried to loop and loop.
He had much fun and many a fright—
This is the tale of Cruncher's flight.

Children's
POOLBEG